Poems from a Stagecoach

Madeleine Snook

BookLeaf Publishing

Presentation by *BookLeaf Publishing*

Web: www.bookleafpub.com

E-mail: info@bookleafpub.com

ISBN: 9789357440899

First edition 2023

To every twenty-something year old scared of the future, struggling to climb the corporate ladder, to get a foot in the door, to find a safe space to truly be yourself, or make a meaningful mark in the world, this is for you.

PREFACE

The following were written on the bus, in the quiet hours at work, and on my tiny bedroom floor on scraps of paper and on the notes app of my phone as I went to work, back home, and to bed for 21 days in that order.

They are the culmination of my thoughts and emotions for years or just for the day, which in any other art form I have not been able to express.

I wrote these in a time of worrying instability and emerging new frontiers- the last half of my twenties- as my cathartic outlet.

I hope at least one other person may find solace, contemplation, or enjoyment in these poems. If so, my job will be done.

Bongo

you have but one chance
how shall we do this dance
monkey your paw chained to the bongo taut
keep tapping, tapping, tapping
in time you'll suck the toes of incessant throws
duck, swim with the current crashing
behind, stay slick and afloat with the oil
that coats the plume, the pen, the cache, the coin
pigs who puff on the steam of your sweat
and whet the grinding gears with tears
from tears in hand, in heart, and sole
no stopping, limp on
dog, we mustn't bare our teeth
the mark of insanity's not a scream but a smile
all the while the ticker thunders, sputters, rattles
snake, fear the chariot of Time, it draws near
wheels trundling, trundling, trundling,
bundle yourself in a crack in the wall
and like a spore grow more
kill for the crevice, the foothold, the gap
crab, scuttle sideways never forward,
onward to a larger shell
settle, fill, settle, fill
a bell chimes in the wake
of the weak wave of respite

‘Goodnight’ the bright light blinds
vitamins, painkillers, coffee beans
trickle down the gullet, you see,
gull, early for the worm you’re asleep
on your feet, head down and start pecking
the screen, the keyboard, the pin code, the plate
too late you were born
on a bough already torn

Solve

Doctor, I'm tired
The car alarms
Salves for sleep- lavender balm

The air is black
My brain is fog
Solve for x, then find the log

Houses on fire
Put out the flames
Save up for a rainy day

Waters rising
The floods sunk all
Sieve for gold before the fall

Pause

I saw a man on the phone
Walking towards me alone
He scuffed at something on the street
It was deliberate and it was brief
I pause a beat to see the heap
Of crumpled feathers and a beak

By the cathedral wall
Inchoately small
But a foot barred from the burying green
O'er the stone I could see
On concrete to decay for days and weeks

How this masterpiece came to be thrown
Like waste discarded on the road
Rubbish, butts and cans, things of man
Fitting in the palm of my hand
I'll never understand

Though by a mother born
From a womb you weren't torn
Of precious porcelain untouched by thumbs
That most delicate, opulent ovum
Through rushing rain and wailing winds did not succumb

A wonder- and with pine and thunder
For Abraxas, cracked the world asunder
And in the sounds that yolk did soak
Scattered cries and creaking oak
Never bore it fruit to croak

Nay, in months Mozart could never fathom
A sweeter pair of cords in tandem
To salute the Sun with sintering song
As bright as a bell in the hum of the throng
As languid as is long

What befell you in this place here
O Dear, my eyes smart and tear
Does he know that in the dewy dawn
A voice, a sound will be silent, gone?
He talks and walks on- but I will mourn

Shift

Silence is deafening and must be drowned
Fill a mouth-shaped void with any sound
A voice not made by vocal chords
But synthetic sets of circuit boards
I talk aloud to no one- the time
Being we three: me, myself and I dine
together of a night, me thinks, I see, Good, myself?
Single servings made for health

I glide by the street as a fleeting shadow, a breeze, a sigh
But I'm alive- I dent the light
They say Loneliness grows like a mould
unchecked, uncontrolled around you, cold
And taints the air, your speech, your tread
Like lead being slowly fed
To the waters of your well
Your belly, to seethe and gel

But I see a tunnel twisting before me
A brick building every second slowly
The end is bright, I see my friends
My loves and laughter at the end
I move towards the bright sunlight

And sense the ceiling cease, alight

But take warning, don't heed
For the tunnel, like a seed,
Is ever growing, caressing your back
Halt and peer down at your tracks
Take a look at your ground
And you will have found
The tunnel outpacing, consuming
The stygian dark floods, looming

Outside sounds muffled and meager
Dwindling away but you're eager
To run, to chase, the ombre outpace
But breath is waning in this space
You bang the walls to shock and shout
In hope of help of breaking out
Of a hand extending through the gap
To take yours and mend your map

When no arm comes, no thumbs, no palm
Onwards along the sideline calm
You must go with hope
And in the end at last elope

With a hug and tearful cheer
You shift near and ask in their ear
'Why didn't you hear me?
A sorrowed tear you start to see

Before the answer tart and true
'I was in a tunnel too'

Jewel

My skin in the mirror of a morn
Meets me ragged, rough, forlorn
Like a glove most unloved but still unduly worn

What would I do if my pimples were jewels?
Mine them all with diamanté tools
Or wear them proudly as paparazzi pool
Around me

O if my face was as ornate as sliced agate
Or marble sanded smooth suffice to satiate
A single stone for Michelangelo's gate?

If I could pick the pockets of this pumice store
And pilfer pennies, pounds, and more
No longer would it feel a chore
To wage this war on this banal battlefield
Bubbling with bullets and craters congealed
A carapace, a husk, a rind unpeeled

Sapphires for scars and diamonds for dents
Enough to bargain a bourgeois rent
If scaly crust were crystals set in silver capsules
bent
And wrought as fine as lines of spun gold

My mask would glitter, glean from the mould
To never tarnish or rust in old
Age becomes the one
Who fickle Chance's favour won
Or failing, paid a prince's sum
We say
But I would welcome wrinkles, sags to stay
If in their day silky satin were exchanged

Suite

In hours idly standing by
When days are long and doorbells sigh
When teardrops prick the puffy eyes
Velum aching, acrid, dry
I think of amber eyes that verify
A humble honey heart
The purest love to ever stand apart
From speech or act or art

Undeserved for such devotion
Deep and vast, a steadfast ocean
Our kind accepts, receives the motion
But failing to return the notion
Only bathes and basks this balmy lotion
A single lifetime of service and action
From birth to death is but a fraction

Of time for human toes
To run and jump and bend and grow
On Earth, it must be so
To smile then suffer and find another to know
Too briefly until the time to go
Again, that nose the first to tell
To search, to sniff, to sense, to smell

That lolling tongue to lap and lick
At moment's quip to briskly wick
Away the flame of fury, hurt, or sick
In barest air a ticking tail quick
To dance and glance a glow euphoric
In plainest gaiety this suite of features meet
The burning return of weary feet
Fawning adoring, gallop to greet

And in that union at the crest
Embrace the one that knows me best
What fate were fingers shaped for lest
On heads or hinds caress and rest?
These feelings, friends, so sacred, blessed
Give gratitude and thanks for sharing time
Within this carnal world, canine divine

Dough

My belly rumbles
I knead the dough in my palm
It rises again

Acorn

In the dark small hours I dread, abhor
The leaden slumber sliced asunder
My spine, my core, my feet are sore
I implore, please
Please let me lie for a minute more
Ere the rising Sun and strident roar
Of my curtain call

Instant coffee acrid as acorns
To oil the clunky cogs from ear to tear
I pull myself down the street with oars
Like a marionette on a string each foot flopping,
limbs lolling
Head bobbing on my chest
Trying to keep abreast
And surface, heave a breath

Some omnipresent puppeteer
Commandeering this somnolent ship
Steers me here and there without a care
With glazed button eyes and cellophane hands
They stand me wobbling on the spot
An automaton at your service
Impervious, despondent

A record's quarter clipped and buffering
Plays the same tune stuttering
My jukebox distant echoing
In my empty skull reverberating
Do these do that do be do am-
Do these people know the air is water
Do they see me wade to wander yonder?

Let me row my boat gently
And jetty on the haven I crave
At the crepuscule at last
I hasten to fasten myself in sheets
To cease, to crop, to stop
Don't bother singing siren
I'm floating, floundering, drowning in your bay

The bray in the sound alarms me
Awake to start the day again

Trait

There once was a sexist, A. Tate
Who flexed with his terrible trait
Some thirty-three cars
Now he's behind bars
In a shiny Romanian crate

Clock

When forests clock a verdant hue
And creatures stir and chirp and mew
When bushes hum with hidden hives
And breezes teem with scents alive
Think brightly of the butterfly
Why does it fly? From whence it came?
In answer lies a Deathly Dame
Who, slaying, makes fine Summer drown
Beneath a carpet rusty brown
She takes her crown and walks on ice
A flower gown her prized device

A floret flashing every shade
Through cherry, maple, oak arcades
She wades as such so simple sweet
Until a time should she so meet
A swarthy figure in the white
Who follows 'spite her hardest might
In blackened robes the pearly bones
They rattled so like falling stones
Skirting along the water's edge
She falters at the darkest ledge

And cutting up a deadly blow
His slicing scythe did reap to sow

Scattered roses, posies, peonies
In thawing grounds- gorge to eyrie
But from the reaper's violent swipe
Went petals flying with the knife
To flutter, torn, two piece abreast
And seldom settle, cease, arrest
With legs of thread on rooted looms
To sew their soles in kindred blooms

And in the night up higher, still
Flung farther than the fairest hill
The gems of Winter's broken crown
Inset, embedded, shining down
Guide Her motley sombre mantle
Those who dither, dance to candles
Come thither to Her diamond jewels
And knit together floral spools
To weave a woman never worn
And sleep once more 'till Springtime's dawn

Trunk

What be the purpose of a human hand

If not to gently reach and blushing, brand

The mark of trust, affection, both withstand?

This question baldly being my demand

I float untethered through the thronging crowd

Alone to weave around the trunks of shirts

Who seem to be a copse as still as loud

Except a fuming fir may do no hurt

At least, at best, I may embrace a tree

And freely take my arms about its waist

Create a sample scene to daily dream

Of feeling warmth between my fingers laced

Until that day I sing this sole etude

Of touch as sore a need as sleep or food

Heath

A many year has since become to pass
Those hardened winter months at last to wilt
Upon the dawn of Spring and songbirds' lilt
There whence I walked upon Dùn Èideann's
grass

A tender treeling cradled in my arms
A switch of hazel most precarious
A slim and shaking sapling tremulous
In nothing save a pot of simple charm

And there atop that southern slope to bear
The city drums a distant hum, a haze
I take my spade and set your name, Calltainn
Departing thus with care I leave you there

Forsooth, I hope that when we meet again
Up high a hill in Pentland's windswept heath
I'll find not twigs nor cloven prints of thieves
And circling, wandering long, then homewards
head
You'll see me pass without a glance instead
There proudly on the edge to Wild append

Swell

Stirring in the pregnant wind the plastic paper drifts
Like jellyfish in the current rift
Translucent spirits dip and shift
And haunt all wheres unwelcome to dwell
The ghosts of gulls whose bellies swell
With grits and chips of L'Oreal
Pumps and chunks they couldn't spew
A sordid confetti to sand anew
Debris to sweep inside in lieu

We're shitting the bed
And lying content instead
In new comfort, our daily bread
Three seconds of life in spite defies to die
Feigns a death dissolving, again arise
Ne'er depart the cave but dormant lies
Inside no brick to build organic forms
Nor sculpt the wind or bubbling storms
Nor guide the daylight to sojourn

But like a septic seed no green to sprout
It rots the fruit from inside out
The flesh decays and melts away
This germ, eternal, sits to stay,

Then bides its time
This enzyme
Of death

Cause

‘You’ve got a little pot belly’
She said, a rerun of the telly
Suck in your uterus to fit in, insert
The trousered role, the rich man’s skirt
He modelled off a paper mannequin
Simply fold into a ramekin
Out of sight and out of mind
Maximise standing space and shrink in kind
Excuse me.

‘You gotta give a man a child- it's the best thing you'll ever do’
Don’t take it that way, don’t be rude
And smile too, it’s all in jest
Dream and be anything if you try your best
Then settle for a modicum, a meagre cut
And saunter where cocks strut
I study, practice, plan, myself believe
I play, I write, I score, invent, achieve
Excuse me?

‘Learn to drive, you stupid bitch!’
He stalked me to the car park to satisfy that itch
An ego tissue thin, a boiling tender gel
Encased within an automotive shell

A minor tremor to crack the kind veneer
And return a tsunami from a single tear
What did I do to cause
Such inflammatory flaws?
Excuse me!

'Oh, so beautiful!' He gasped
As he reached toward my face to tear off my
mask
I step away with tasteful grace
And therein lies my gross mistake
No needs neither language nor lungs
And so transcends foreign tongues
No police appear for predators' pursuits
Just forgive and forget? There is nothing to
Excuse you

Stamp

Every time I see that meat
Cooking in inferno's heat
Seared and stamped behind my eyes
Grisly pictures play, arise

Pinned and shackled
Baby cattle
Footsteps looming
Chains are rattled

Pounding, punching
Sounds of thudding
Dollish faces
"Tenderising"

Chickens fatten
Growing sudden
Bony femurs
Snap and flatten

Ankles clamping
Thrashing slashing
Upside-downward
Trundle, bashing

Piglets squirming
Pliers worming
Open wider
Bleeding, burning

Crying mother
Someplace other
Crushed in boxes
Squealing, smothered

Cower cornered
Lambs for slaughter
Bash the button
Draw and quarter

Greasy fingers
Slick and limber
Sliding, sucking
Slip and linger

Cruelly cracking
Shinbone snapping
Slurping, burping
Coughing, hacking

Get your cutlet
Trough or bucket?
Live without me
Chicken nuggets?

‘Tis the season!
Little reason
Something fed and
Someone eaten

Chomping on, you chew the fat
Tearing tendons where you sat
Crunching on the crusted carcass
Battered body skinned and heartless

Mouse

A cute house pops up
I move the mouse and hover
Bother. Baked bean dreams

Quiet

At night I fax myself to bed
Then print a board and forth I tread
With bones that rattle, creak, and crack
A xylophone, I play my back
My fingers pop like bubble wrap
And bending low I hear a snap
A crunchy neck atop a set
Of shoulders wound with springs of frets
This body nearly thirty years
Should be so wrought with rusty gears?

I wish that at my fateful death
I take another kind of breath
Of all the creatures on this earth
But one to be and give rebirth
To heavens I will not ascend
But downwards to a sweeter end
To leave this land, return instead
An octopus to live ahead

No bone to break or fracture save
My mouth to masticate enclaved
And squeezing though the tightest gap
Emerge unharmed in mind and clap
My tentacles the only knots

In flesh to weave themselves besot
Adorned with fourfold hands although
No work awaits, nor trickling dough
No papers pushed nor buttons too
They kneel in rows beneath my shoes

With wise ram eyes to scan the sea
Beyond imagination see
All colours, textures sing and dance
I'll change my mantle at a glance
And with a pulsing puzzling wit
I'll play with sharks and forth-ward flit
Away the day as fit for kings
And dine on shellfish surfeiting
If I should bleed a royal blue
I'll grow another arm anew

Then flying freely through that space
I'll feel the water's quiet embrace
Above, below, a weighted wool
To wrap around without a pull
If ending not atop the plate
An undulating life awaits

Faith

What faith I had is all but gone
Our leaders talk and carry on
Like usual business nothing's done
The smoke is growing by the tonne
Those polar bears all swim for land
With rising water eating sand
The last of forests slashed and burned
Within the time the Earth has turned
Two hundred species by the day
Forever gone and wiped away
The sacred rivers of our past
Now black and belching up the last
Society's detritus dumped
There out of sight in stinking slums
Away from sprawling shopping malls
Fluorescents stalls consuming all
For every comfort, any way
A lengthy price we'll shortly pay
Clear the woods and raise a herd
To feed the world but waste a third
All piled up high and left to rot
Carbon dioxide
Three hundred and fifty gigatonnes
And less left to pollute
The clock is ticking, left on mute

67 percent of chance to live
With doing all we can give
1.5 degrees Celsius
Of global temperature increase
O n e p o i n t f i v e d e g r e e s
Before a chain reaction seismic
Irreversible and cataclysmic-
Oh my god!
Did Kim have an affair?
Who cares? One point five degrees before-
Jobs and growth with increased savings
As I was saying,
If we unite together and persuade
The leaders who still haven't made-
Thoughts and prayers for flooded cities
One point five degrees-
You know it's all a conspiracy, right?
The science is final- we need to act
It's time for fear, and swift react-
Is the dress white and gold or blue and black?

I'm done with talking.
I'm out and walking.

Do
Something
Now.

I'm done.

Boots

Best of all to guide my bearing
Waiting in my wardrobe ready
Boots- a pairing
Slumping in perfection steady

Blackened once but now since faded
Scuffed in places, scenes of anguish
Feeling, aided
Bearing brunts they lean and languish

Buckles tarnished over Winters,
Sunken seats, cathedrals spiring
Soles have splintered
Chasing something all inspiring

Years, a decade surplus serving
Moulding to my rolling ankles
So deserving
Twice a cobbler's door-chime jangles

I'll revive them three times over
Bearing not to part or purchase
Brand leftover
Quelling sentimental urges

Sleep

In liminal space of sleep and wake
The Ancient Hive neither one nor many
A Mind submerged, incorporeal
Finer than a spider's web
Teething tendrils will find the threads
And grasping, tentatively, bind
Adjoin the cradling bosom
A droplet in a cloud
A neuron in the brain
A grain of the sand
The first to tread on inchoate land
Yet only known a stranger
Plant in semblance something gorm
But like a beast devours the form
The nebulae of space mirrored in the turf
A fabric cloven into Heavens and Earth

In the blustering breeze
The leaves of trees may dance and sing
In loams long settled
Racines will murmur
And whisper songs of seeping streams
Babbling tales in dulcet tones
Humming with Summer's chirping hymns
Weeping for the sawing dead
And crying fire infernos red

All is circled joy and pain
Infirm and infant fed the slain
Consuming fruits of dampened shades
Bounties blooming in darkest days
Taken which was given, sowed
In soundless slumber return what's owed
No box however strong or thick,
Plain or gilded
There is no wall but only hills
For friends of time
Irrevocable, inevitable- it climbs
Dissolves the one to many
So many becomes the one

Wagon

There once was a woman who waited
For a bus already ill-fated
'It's quarter to nine'
'It's never on time'
How long it will be she debated

There once was a wagon that crawled
Alongside the traffic that stalled
'Fuck it, I'll walk'
'Ring work and talk'
That woman decided appalled

There once was a cloud that came
To the bus stop and started to rain
'Is it cancelled or not?'
'Did the driver get shot?'
So long she had waited in vain

There once was a furious girl
Whose fists had started to curl
'How dare they do this!'
She said with a hiss
'I wait like a piteous churl!'

There once was a bus that came
Along that familiar lane
‘Thank god, it’s here’
But past it veered
Tomorrow it’ll be the same

www.ingramcontent.com/pod-product-compliance
Lightning Source LLC
Chambersburg PA
CBHW051745130826
49812CB00033B/1007
* 9 7 8 9 3 5 7 4 4 0 8 9 9 *